FUN FACTS

RIPLEY'S
Believe It or Not!®
Kids

& SILLY STORIES

1

Consultant Camilla de la Bedoyere
Design Rocket Design
Reprographics Juice Creative

Published by Ripley Publishing 2015
Ripley Publishing, Suite 188, 7576 Kingspointe Parkway,
Orlando, Florida 32189, USA

10 9 8 7 6 5

ISBN 978-1-60991-054-9 (US)

Library of Congress Cataloging-in-Publication Data

Fun facts and silly stories.
    p. cm. -- (Ripley's believe it or not!)
  ISBN 978-1-60991-054-9
1. Curiosities and wonders--Juvenile literature.
 AG243.F855 2012
 031.02--dc23

                        2012024617

Manufactured in China
in April/2015
5th printing

WARNING
Some of the stunts and activities in this book are
undertaken by experts and should not be attempted
by anyone without adequate training and supervision.

First published in Great Britain in 2013 by
Random House Books, Random House,
20 Vauxhall Bridge Road, London SW1V 2SA

www.randomhouse.co.uk

Addresses for companies within The Random House
Group Limited can be found at
www.randomhouse.co.uk/offices/htm

The Random House Group Limited Reg. No. 954009

A CIP catalogue record for this book is available from
the British Library

ISBN 9780099568049 (UK)

For information regarding permission, write to VP
Intellectual Property, Ripley Entertainment Inc., Suite
188, 7576 Kingspointe Parkway, Orlando, Florida 32819
Email: publishing ripleys.com
www.ripleybooks.com

PUBLISHER'S NOTE
While every effort has been made to verify the accuracy
of the entries in this book, the Publishers cannot be held
responsible for any errors contained in the work. They
would be glad to receive any information from readers.

FUN FACTS

Ripley's Believe It or Not! Kids

& SILLY STORIES

1

Question:
When is a sardine
not a sardine?

Answer:
When it gets together with thousands of friends to make a giant dolphin!

This huge school of sardines in the shape of a dolphin was snapped by a photographer in the Philippines. It is made up of thousands of sardines that group together for protection from predators.

CROCS EAT ROCKS!

A bellyful of stones helps them digest food and stay underwater.

Turtles can breathe through their butts

Although turtles breathe using their lungs like most animals, they also have a pair of sacs in their butt that take in water and extract oxygen from it. So, they really can "breathe through their butts".

Look guys, pretty bubbles!

8

horses
do not
vomit

Horses have a very strong muscle at the top of their stomach that closes after food is swallowed. It acts as a one-way route that lets food go down, but not come back up again.

9

KANGAROOS
don't move backward.

They can only jump, not walk!

A poison dart frog has enough poison to kill

10 people.

Dogs sweat through their feet
—most of their sweat glands are on their paw pads.

can COWS climb ladders?

LADDER SHOULD BE LEANED AGAINST A SOLID, NON-MOVING OBJECT

ALWAYS HAVE A FRIEND SUPPORTING THE BOTTOM OF THE LADDER

NEVER LEAN TOO FAR TO THE SIDE WHEN ON A LADDER

Believe it or not, this poor creature got his head stuck between the rungs of a ladder! An animal inspector managed to free him and return him safely to his herd.

OTHER COWS NOT HELPING

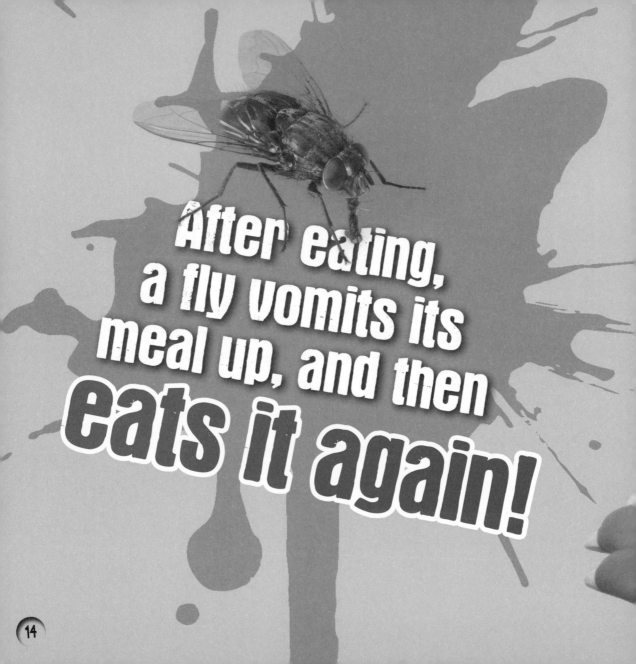

After eating, a fly vomits its meal up, and then eats it again!

NO WEIGH!

Milly is quite possibly the smallest dog in the world. She stopped growing at three months, and weighs just under 6 ounces (170 g).

Chihuahuas usually reach a height of 6 to 10 inches (15 to 25 cm) but Milly measures just 2½ inches (6.5 cm) tall.

It's a Dog-Lion-Zebra

Dog grooming is taken to the extreme in some contests in the U.S.A. The pampered pets are clipped, brushed, and dyed to look like other creatures or even movie characters. Some have been transformed to look like horses, lions, zebras, pandas, or a mix of animals.

Lobsters have blue BLOOD.

Cut here

Cockroaches can live for a week without their head.

More people are TRAMPLED to death by cows than are killed by sharks.

19

Earthworms have **FIVE** hearts.

The heart of a blue whale is the size of a small car.

It beats nine times a minute. A human heart beats around 70 times a minute.

PYGMY HIPPO POO CAN FLY!

The animals swirl their tail around when they poo. This flings the poo around to mark their territory.

21

THE WOOLLY

BEFORE

Shrek the sheep hid in caves in New Zealand for six years so by the time his coat was eventually cut it weighed 60 pounds (27 kg)!

MAMMOTH

AFTER

A snail produces such a thick layer of slime that it could crawl over a razor blade without damaging itself.

A RAT CAN GNAW THROUGH ALMOST ANYTHING.

They cause a quarter of electric cable breaks and nearly as many problems with phone lines.

Rats eat or spoil around ONE FIFTH of the world's food every year.

Believe it or not, goats can climb trees! They climb up argan trees, found mostly in Morocco, because they like to eat the fruit, which is similar to an olive.

must be kidding!

Some sharks walk on their fins underwater.

A sailfish can leap through the air at 68 mph. (109 km/h)

Elephants
produce around
200 pounds
(90 kg)
of poo every day.

Heads up!

The peacock mantis shrimp has front legs strong enough to smash **BULLETPROOF GLASS!**

HOPPING

MAD

Rabbit jumping is a crazy new sport that began in Scandinavia and can now be found all around the world. The ideal jumping rabbit has long legs and a long back. Champions can clear fences that are over 3 feet high (1 m), and can jump up to 10 feet (3 m) in the long-jump competition.

concentrate!

legs tucked well in

awesome "big air"

check out one of my classic "text book" jumps... Look and learn!

1,000,000 locusts make a swarm!

STARFISH CAN REGROW LOST ARMS

Sometimes a whole new starfish will grow from just one severed arm and part of the central body!

Spiders' brains are so LARGE that they run all the way down into their legs.

LUCKY DUCKY

Lucky the duckling can walk again after being fitted with a duck shoe! The specially made sandal helped her leg to heal after she broke it.

BOING!

Scarlett, a piglet from England, just loves the trampoline! The piglet's secret skill was discovered when her owners put her on their daughters' trampoline.

Daddy, is it my turn yet?

Brrrr!

These swallows in Canada are keeping each other warm in a snowstorm. They fluff up their feathers and huddle together to share body heat.

actual size!

THE AMERICAN BULLFROG TADPOLE CAN MEASURE 6.75 INCHES LONG!

(17.2 cm)

your "regular" tadpole

The call of an American bullfrog is so low it sounds like the mooing of a cow!

Some jellyfish eat their own babies.

Cows, dogs, and birds can have different accents, depending on where they live.

Fish scales are used to make lipstick shimmer.

Pucker up!

These chickens were almost bald when they were rescued from factory farms in England. Animal welfare officers kept them warm by dressing them in these bright sweaters, or "chickinis".

Alright darling?

cock-a-doodle ladies!

Newborn Galapagos tortoises are 3,000 times smaller than their mothers!

565 pounds
(256 kg)

3 ounces
(87 g)

This little guy will take 30 years to get to the same size as its mother.

SPARE PARTS

The glass lizard has no legs and sometimes no tail! If the lizard is attacked, its tail breaks off and wriggles away to trick the attacker.

Dogs pant up to 300 times a minute.

Phew, it's hot in here!

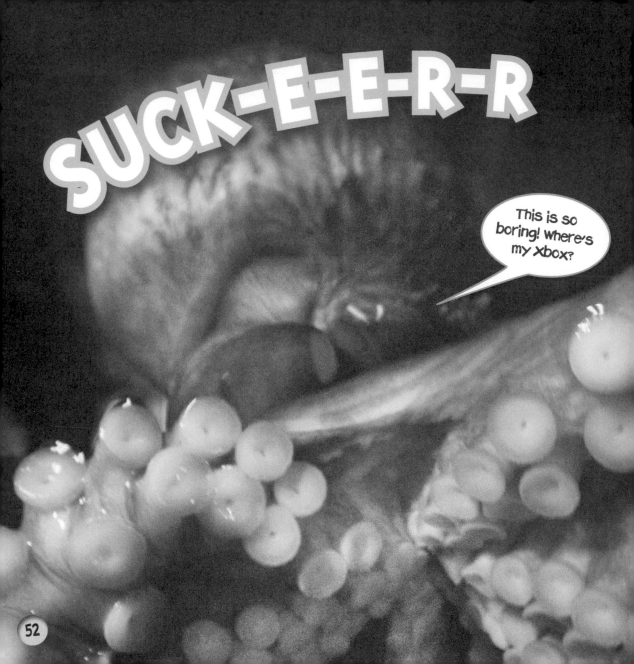

Scientists gave 25 octopuses Rubik's Cubes to play with to see which tentacle they liked to use to pick things up.

the weight of ants in the world =

the weight of people in the world

SQUEEZE!

Ksyusha the kitten can climb in and out of some tight places including this jar! She started climbing into jars when she was a few weeks old, and now hides in all sorts of places, including the washing machine!

Срок годности 1 год при температуре от +2°С до +25°С и относительной влажности воздуха не более 75%.
Дата изготовления:

СЛИВОВЫЙ

Here Kitty Kitty!

THORNY BUGS

Believe it or not, these spiky looking thorns are actually female thorn bugs feeding on a tree branch. Great camouflage!

A gecko can hang from a ceiling with just ONE toe.

An octopus has **THREE** hearts.

Cuttlefish can change their patterns many times every second.

SEEING RED

This flock was painted red to cheer up people driving past a farmer's field in Scotland! Sometimes farmers dye their sheep to help count them, or to stop them from being stolen.

Who's a pretty boy then?

Whipper the budgie is not like other budgies. He suffers from "feather duster" disease, which means he grows extra long feathers that fluff up like a feather duster!

SHARP SHOOTER!

Aiiieee!

Archerfish catch their prey by squirting water! They usually hit the target, which can be up to 5 feet (1.5 m) away, with their first shot. If the prey is close to the water, the fish can even leap out to grab it with its mouth.

Gotcha!

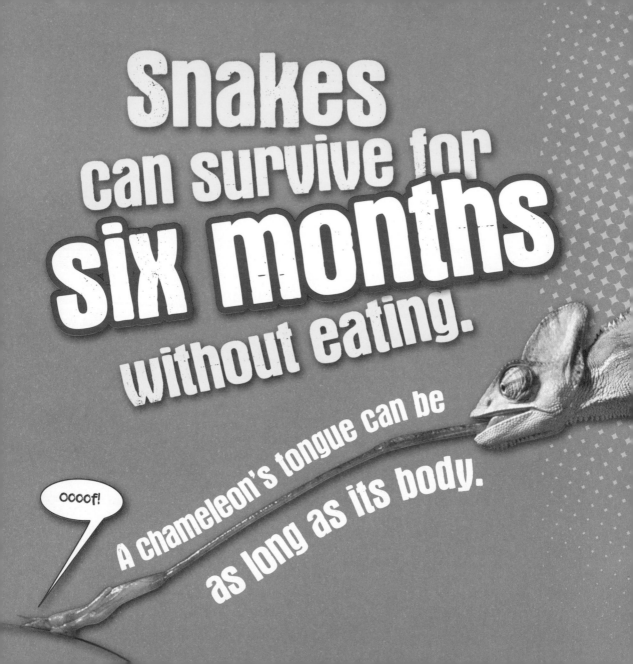

A RHINO'S SKIN IS OFTEN THICKER THAN A HUMAN WRIST.

Damselflies have two **HUGE** eyes that are made up of about 30,000 lenses.

The oldest **goldfish** on record was **over 40** years old.

An elephant's trunk has more than 40,000 muscles.

SUPER-GOO

Parrotfish blow their own bubble of goo to protect themselves at night. It keeps away parasites that bite them and suck their blood.

A bee produces only half a teaspoon of honey during its lifetime.

A giant squid has teeth...

...in its tentacles!

The tentacles grab its prey and the teeth grip it so it can't escape.

Awesome!

MR. GREEDY!

Male gorillas can eat over 40 pounds (18 kg) of grass, leaves, and roots a day. That's the same as you eating

500

bags of potato chips.

Phaaarp!

74

GREAT WHITE SHARKS

CAN ROLL THEIR EYES

BACK IN THEIR HEAD FOR PROTECTION.

Giraffes and mice both have seven bones in their neck.

ELEPHART!

Five is an artistic elephant who lives at a safari park in the U.K. She has painted more than 50 beautiful pictures by holding the brush in her trunk.

HIPPOS
ARE COVERED IN
RED SLIME!

Their skin produces
rosy-red goo, which acts
as a sunblock.

Kangaroos are
good swimmers!

Geckos lick their eyes to keep them clean!

This is because most of them don't have eyelids.

MEET THE FUNNIES
Introducing a few of nature's jokers...

Wow, check out that mohawk!

Eucharitid wasp

Elvis bug

Monkey grasshopper

Has somone been messing about with the highlighter pen?

81

Spiders spun some amazing webs when escaping from floods in Australia. As the waters rose, the spiders scuttled out of the way, climbing up trees and bushes spinning their webs as they went.

NON-SLIP SLIPPERS

I can't believe we both bought the same slippers!

Polar bears' feet have thick tufts of fur, strong claws, and little bumps to stop them from sliding on the ice!

GOTCHA!

Net-casting spiders spin a web of thick silk, which they use as a net to throw over their prey.

A new born joey (baby kangaroo) is so small it could fit into this teaspoon.

A **squirrel** in the U.K. squeezed inside a bird feeder and ate so many peanuts it couldn't get back out between the bars!

Anteaters are able to stick out their tongues up to **160** times a minute.

SPLIT ENDS

Lambada
is a Baudet de
Poitou donkey,
which is a rare
species that grows
lovely long locks!
They are one of the oldest
donkey species, and only
50 of them are born each year.

SOME CATS HAVE FOUR EARS!

This is very unusual and the cats cannot hear through their extra ears. They are really just ear-flaps!

Pardon?

Sperm whales are often scratched and scarred by fights with their largest prey, the giant squid and the colossal squid.

HALF-PIPE HOUND!

Tillman the bulldog loves to ride his skateboard around his home city of Los Angeles. He plays on the ramps in skate parks and can also ride down stairs. Tillman even has his own line of hats and t-shirts.

Barracudas
keep fish prisoner
if they aren't hungry enough
to eat them straightaway.

Sea urchins can walk on their TEETH!

Fishermen in Chesapeake Bay were amazed when they spotted a whitetail deer swimming in water 80 feet (24 m) deep

1½ miles (2.4 km)

from shore. They lassoed it, lifted it into the boat, and took it back to dry land.

BRRRRRR!
(how not to make snowballs)

Kenzie the terrier couldn't wait
to play out in the snow,
but look what happens
when furry feet get frozen!
It's OK, one warm bath later
and Kenzie's paws were
defrosted and
back to normal.

SOME CATERPILLARS HAVE 12 EYES.

Each head of a rare two-headed snake can fight over food.

GONE WITH THE WIND

When a storm struck Michigan, a 5-pound (2.3-kg) Chihuahua called Tinkerbell was picked up by a gust of wind and blown away. She was discovered unharmed two days later half a mile away in a forest.

PARA PUG

Otis is a pug in a parachute that just loves to freefall! He wears special "doggles" to protect his eyes, and makes each jump in a harness strapped to his owner. He has been jumping for nine years and loves it.

Rascal, a Chinese crested pure breed, won California's ugly dog contest.

Nancy the cat has been nicknamed "the gremlin".

ooooh, look at those evil eyes!

BiG mama

Wolf spiders carry their babies on their back!

Insects don't have blood. They are filled with a

GREEN

or yellow goo!

CATS ALWAYS WALK ON **TIPTOE.**

Wildlife experts dress up in giant panda costumes to look after panda cubs.

WHY?

These cubs in China will be released into the wild when they are ready. They need to have as little human contact as possible, so their keepers put on the costumes whenever they need to handle the cubs.

BALD EAGLES

CAN SWIM!

A shark cannot move if it is flipped upside down.

yup, I can't move.

Could someone help take our hats off?

QUACKERS!

Visitors to the Sydney Family Show in Australia can watch ducks wearing dresses, hats, and ball gowns. The grand finale of the fashion show features a duck bride and groom in full wedding gear!

Cows produce more milk when listening to music.

Ribbon worms can eat 95 percent of their own bodies if they cannot find food—and still survive!

DOG-GONE!

A four-year-old boy from England decided his week-old cocker spaniel needed a bath, so he put the dog in the toilet and flushed it! Plumbers found and rescued the tiny puppy in a waste pipe 20 yards (20 m) from the house.

Poor pup!

To boldly go where no chicken has gone before!

A rubber chicken called Camilla was sent into space in a spaceship made from a lunchbox! She was attached to a helium balloon and launched by students from a school in California as part of an experiment to study weather in space. After 2½ hours, the balloon popped and Camilla parachuted safely back to Earth.

Camilla before her epic trip

BAT WRAPS

ZZZZZZ

These baby bats were kept warm in little blankets after being rescued from the wild in Australia. A special bat nursery was set up to save baby bats who had been made orphans after serious floods in the area.

CLUMSY APES!

Approximately 50 percent of orangutans have **BROKEN BONES.** This is because they often fall out of trees.

120

A starfish can poke its own STOMACH OUT through its mouth to eat.

No way!

Snails can sleep for three to four years at a time.

A group
of penguins on land
is called a **waddle.**

Some seals sleep for only 90 seconds at a time.

Polar bears can **smell humans** from 20 miles (32 km) away.

Moles can dig 75 feet (22 m) of tunnels in a day.

PURRFECT
LUXURY

Craig Grant built a 30-acre (12 ha) cat sanctuary in Florida. It has cat-sized buildings including a city hall and police station! Caboodle Ranch is now home to 660 happy cats.

A lion's canine teeth can grow up to **3 INCHES** (7.5 cm) long!

A python can swallow a **whole** kangaroo.

woooaah, indigestion!

When a Jack Russell terrier chewed up the mail at his home in England, the chewed glue and paper stuck his jaws together!

129

SWOOOOSH!

c-c-can't stop!

Rollie the penguin liked skating so much he joined the National Rollerskating Association!

SQUELCH!

Schoolgirl Tiana Walton from England let 25 snails slither across her face. The nine-year-old said she found it relaxing, but the snails were a bit cold and smelly—and she could see their long eyes looking at her.

Two baby owls have found new homes in kitchen cups! The six-week-old owlets, named Linford and Christie, have moved in with wildlife park keeper Jimmy Robinson who is hand-rearing them at his home in England. They also like hiding in the dog basket and the bookcase!

Nice cup!

BEES CANNOT FLY WHEN IT RAINS.

A garden snail would take 95 YEARS to slide around the world. Garden snails move at a pace of ½ inch per second (13 mm/sec) and are the fastest snail movers.

DEER ME!

Connie Beck woke one morning to hear strange noises in her home in Pennsylvania. When she went to look, she found a deer taking a bubble bath in the bathtub! Not only had the deer broken into the house, it had also managed to turn on the water, knock over a bottle of bubble bath, and climb into the tub!

THEY'RE NUTS!

Now, which ones are mine?

Acorn woodpeckers spend hours pecking hundreds of holes in tree trunks. They then pick acorns from oak trees and carefully fit them into a hole that's just the right size.

Alligators can be hypnotized

zzzzzz

in 30 seconds by turning them over and putting pressure on their necks.

SHARKS HAVE NO BONES.

PHWOAR!

A spotted skunk often does handstands before it squirts its stinky spray. Its spray can reach up to

15 feet
(4.5 m)

and is used to scare off enemies.

Take that!

TEAM BUILDING!

Ants link together
to make a bridge
so their friends can
cross a gap!

DOLPHIN'S BRIDE!

Believe it or not, Sharon Tendler married Cindy the dolphin at a special ceremony in Israel. She got down on one knee and gave Cindy a kiss and a piece of herring. Sharon and Cindy had known each other for 15 years before their wedding.

The globefish can puff itself up to three times its normal size to scare off attackers. It does this by filling an air bladder inside its body.

A **starving** mouse will eat its own tail.

Giraffes can lick their own ears!
Their tongue is more than 12 inches (30 cm) long.

Boxer crabs have claws that really STING!

HOW COME?

The crab grabs sea anemones and holds them in its front claws as extra weapons to fight off its enemies.

Comin' atcha!

Some fish swim together in huge shoals, or schools, containing thousands of fish.

Stop pushing!

Koalas don't drink

No thanks mate, I don't drink.

WANT TO KNOW WHY?

Koalas hardly ever have to drink because the only food they eat is eucalyptus leaves, which are 50 percent water. They can even tell the age of the leaves by their smell. Eucalyptus is so low in energy that koalas spend 20 hours a day asleep.

SOME FROGS DON'T HAVE EARS

Nope, none on this one

Panamanian golden frogs don't have outside ears—their lungs pick up sound waves and direct them to their eardrums.

A flamingo can only eat when its head is upside down.

A WALRUS has three times the sucking power of a vacuum cleaner. This might explain why its stomach is full of small pebbles!

An earthworm has no eyes, ears, or nose.

MINI MACS

These little lambs needed protection from harsh winter weather, so the farmer dressed them in bright red plastic coats! They helped keep the lambs warm, and scared off predators such as foxes.

LIVING FEAST!

20 million bats live in a cave!

There are so many bats in Bracken Cave, Texas, that it takes more than three hours for them all to leave.

Must fly, don't want to get caught in the evening rush!

Prairie dogs kiss and cuddle when they meet each other.

... but what about me? Always left on my own with nobody to cuddle... sob!

TRUE LOVE?

When angler fish breed, the tiny male fish grabs onto the larger female with its mouth, and never lets go! His body gradually joins with hers and he is stuck there forever!

ouch, stop biting my butt!

FLY SWAT

This impala needs a spring clean! It was caught on camera with a fully-woven spider web stretching between its horns.

There's no flies on me!

PARTNERS

Sea otters hold paws while sleeping to stop them from drifting apart.

When moles eat earthworms, they first squeeze them like a tube of toothpaste to push out their SOILY POO!

Gross!

160

Using its antennae a bee can locate an apple tree three miles (5 km) away.

Lottie the tortoise disappeared from her home in England in 2008. She was found **two years later,** just 1½ miles (2.4 km) away.

Mosquitoes prefer biting people with smelly feet.

She's up!

Ah, so that's why I always get bitten!

SAY WHAT?

Do goats faint? Believe it or not, they do! The fainting goat is a breed that goes stiff and falls over whenever it's startled. It remains still on the ground for about 15 seconds before it jumps up again.

She's up again!

She's down!

Greedy GUTS!

Tiger sharks eat just about anything! Scientists have found all kinds of things inside the stomachs of these scavengers, such as car parts, a roll of chicken wire, a sack of coal, shoes, a tin of Spam, rags, bottles, and even a dog!

BLEURGH

165

DANGER COWS' TONGUES!

Cows caused a lot of damage to a house in Tennessee, just by licking it! They stuck their heads through their fence, which was just a few feet from the home of Jerry Lynn Davis, and broke a gutter and a screen window with their strong tongues.

GIZZA KISS!

A hamster is able to carry half its own bodyweight in food in its cheeks.

cheeky!

One tiny blue-ringed octopus has enough **venom** to **kill** 26 adults.

The nest of a bald eagle can weigh as much as

TWO CARS!

169

A white cat with blue eyes is much more likely to be deaf than other cats.

New balls PLEASE!

ANYONE FOR TENNIS?

Auggie the dog liked to do tricks with tennis balls. Believe it or not, he could pick up FIVE tennis balls in his mouth at the same time!

Spiny lobsters use their long antennae to keep hold of the lobster in front as they march across the seabed. Sometimes more than 50 lobsters join the line to migrate each winter to warmer, calmer waters to lay their eggs.

MEET THE GLOWIES

Deep, deep down on the dark ocean floor...

Cockatoo squid

...some animals create their own light. They use chemicals in their body or cover themselves in light-producing bacteria.

Young gannets are fed so much fish that they are **unable to fly** when leaving the nest.

They **have to starve** for a couple of weeks until they are light enough to take-off.

An octopus has no skeleton and can "ooze" through an opening just bigger than its eyeball.

on your marks, set... GO!

An adult bear can run as fast as a horse!

Ahhh, I see the problem, a bent straw. He's not going to get very far unless...

SHHLURP!

...that's the way, careful now!

When Charlie the chipmunk was thirsty, he decided that a long, cool glass of freshly squeezed orange juice would do very nicely. So, Charlie sucked on the straw before diving head first into the glass and drinking it all!

SHOW OFF!

Forget about the roughness, look at the size of the thing!

Jaguars have rough tongues that are designed to peel the skin away from the flesh of its prey.

A crocodile cannot stick its tongue out.

A wolf's sense of smell is about 100 times better than a human's.

FINE DINING

Red-billed oxpeckers feed from the skin and ears of large African mammals, such as this impala. They like to eat blood-filled ticks, earwax, and snot. Yum!

YUK!

Why did the ducklings think their mother was a white ball?

Mama?

A scientist convinced a group of newborn ducklings that a white ball was their mama because ducklings think that the first moving object they see is their mother.

FANTASY FEST

Dogs were dressed up in some cool outfits for a pet masquerade contest in Florida. Some owners even wore matching costumes.

Really, who ever heard of a dog dressed as a lobster?

DEEP CLEAN

Believe it or not, sea turtles visit underwater cleaning stations to have the algae removed from their shell and body. Schools of fish, such as these yellow tangs, clean up the turtles and send them on their way as good as new!

Hummingbirds are the only birds that can fly backward.

A mouse has 225 bones. A human has only 206.

Dolphins have more teeth than any other mammal. They can have up to 100!

Armadillos can hold their breath for up to six minutes. This means they can stick their nose deep into the ground when hunting insects.

THE GREAT ESCAPE

Step 2
Under cover of darkness, the boys make a run for it.

It's all clear, cover me!

A clever dog was able to free himself and his doggie friends from their kennels at a dogs' home. For several nights, Red the lurcher opened the kennel doors with his nose and teeth. The dogs would then head to the kitchen for snacks, which is where staff found them each morning. Cameras were set up to see how the dogs were escaping, and the game was up.

An average elephant's trunk can hold up to 8½ pints (4 l) of water. An adult male elephant's trunk can hold 21 pints (10 l).

There are more wild pigs than people in Australia. That's 21 million people and 23 million **pigs!**

Centipedes have an odd number of pairs of legs.

DANDY DOLPHIN

I'm one of a kind!

A bright pink albino bottlenose dolphin was spotted in a coastal lake in Louisiana. The dolphin, nicknamed "Pinky," is thought to be the only one of its kind in the world.

A catfish has more than a **quarter of a million** taste buds!

SAY WHAT?

The taste buds are not just in its mouth and gills, but on its whiskers, fins, back, belly, sides, and tail.

MR.BLOBBY

Hmm, I really must tone up.

The **BLOBFISH** lives in deep waters off the southeastern coast of Australia. Sadly, this weird-looking creature is facing extinction.

A CAT in Wales has 26 toes!

That's eight more than normal cats. The cat, named Des, has seven toes on each of his front paws and six on each of his back paws.

A hyena's mouth is so tough that it can chew a GLASS BOTTLE without cutting itself.

Leeches have HUNDREDS of tiny sharp teeth, and 5 pairs of eyes.

Yuk!

PORCUPINES CAN FLOAT IN WATER.

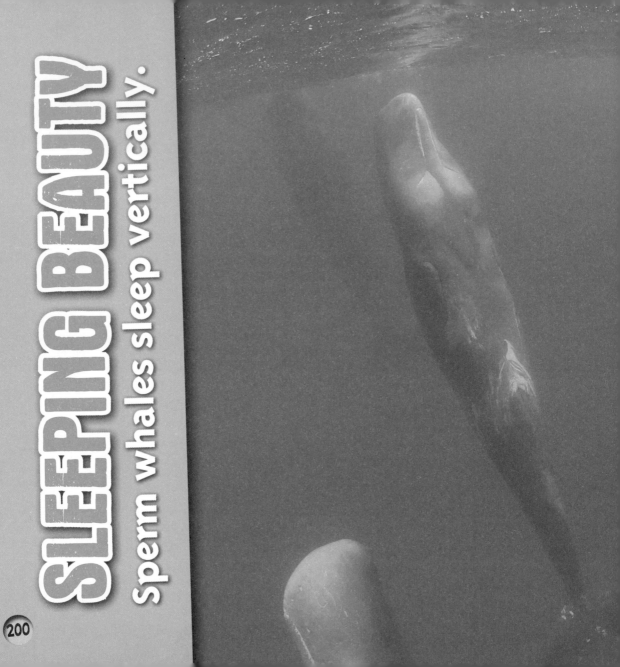

SLEEPING BEAUTY

Sperm whales sleep vertically.

A turtle with green hair?

This little guy was spotted swimming in an Australian river. It's an endangered Mary River Turtle and its crazy green "hair" is actually algae growing on its head.

Australian lyrebirds can imitate almost any sound, including chainsaws, phones, car alarms barking dogs, and **crying babies.**

When four owl chicks were abandoned by their mother, keepers at a wildlife park in England gave them a stuffed toy owl instead. The babies happily snuggled under the toy's wings to keep warm.

YIPPEE!

No prizes for guessing why this little guy is called a

"happy face"

spider! These tiny, rare creatures measure around $1/5$ inch long (5 mm) and are found in Hawaiian rainforests.

BIG MOUTH!

Male jawfish protect their eggs by keeping them inside their enormous mouths.

Sloths EAT, SLEEP, and GIVE BIRTH upside down.

...Which is cool, but when I eat I get crumbs in my eyes!

One pat of elephant dung can contain up to

7,000

dung beetles.

Poo, bit whiffy!

WOW!

More than 307 million ants were once found in a single colony in Japan. There were 45,000 connecting nests built over an area of one square mile (2.5 sq km).

whooo goes there?

Owls have **TEN TIMES** better hearing than you. They can also turn their head up to 270 degrees to help work out exactly where a sound is coming from.

MEET THE BALDIES

Take a deep breath and enter the bald zone...

Reggie, a baby baboon, went bald after his mother licked his head too often!

Spock the Dumbo rat was born bald.

Sphynx cats have no coat at all.

ARACHNID ARMY

Tens of thousands of harvestmen mass together and move as one giant scary creature!

A blue whale's aorta is so wide that an adult human could swim through it.

You would be in deep trouble though!

Aorta = the main artery that supplies blood to the body.

A male African elephant can weigh as much as 100 men!

Believe it or not, POLAR BEARS have black skin!

Honeybees have hairs on their eyes.

INDEX

PHOTO CREDITS

COVER: WestEnd6ı/Rex Features, Gerard Lacz/Rex Features, © Eric Isselée/Fotolia.com

4-5 Steve De Nee/Solent News/Rex Features; 7 © Mammut Vision/Shutterstock.com; 8 (l) © Anteromite/Shutterstock.com (r) Michael S. Nolan/SplashdownDirect/Rex Features; 9 © Studio 37/Shutterstock.com; 10 © MaXPdia/iStock.com; 11 (c/r) © Alfredo Maiquez/iStock.com, (t) © ayzek/Shutterstock.com; 12 (sp) © Eric Isselée/Shutterstock.com, (c) © luchschen/iStock.com; 13 Wenn/SSPCA; 14 (t) © Bogdan Dumitru/Fotolia.com, (c) © Kirsty Pargeter/Shutterstock.com; 15 (b) © NatUlrich/Shutterstock.com, (t) Agencia EFE/Rex Features; 17 Barcroft Media via Getty Images; 18 (b) © Connie Wade/Fotolia.com, (t) © Kirsty Pargeter/Shutterstock.com; 19 © hxdbzxy/Shutterstock.com; 20 (b) © Birsen Cebeci/Shutterstock.com; 22 Ross Land/AP/Press Association Images; 23 AFP/Getty Images; 24 © Ivan Bliznetsov/iStock.com; 25 © Sergey Bolkin/iStock.com; 26 Gavin Oliver/Solent News/Rex Features; 27 © (t/r) Eric Isselée/Shutterstock.com, (c/r) © Jo Lomark/Shuttetstock.com; 28 (l) © Ken Klotz/iStock.com, (r) © Andrey Kasimov/Shutterstock.com; 29 (b) © patrimonio designs limited/Shutterstock.com; 30 © Bernhard Richter/Shutterstock.com; 31 © cosma/Shutterstock.com; 32-33 (sp) Action Press/Rex Features; 33 (t) © Goncharuk/Shutterstock.com; 34-35 Reuters/Juan Medina; 36 © Darren Scanlin/Fotolia.com; 38 Barry Batchelor/PA Archive/Press Association Images; 39 NTI Media Ltd/Rex Features; 40-41 Keith Williams/Solent News/Rex Features; 42 (sp) © Slyers/Shutterstock.com, (t, b) © NHPA/ Joe Blossom; 45 (b) Adam Tinney/Shutterstock.com; 46-47 Albanpix Ltd/Rex Features; 48 Brad Hunter/Newspix/Rex Features; 51 © Justin Horrocks/iStock.com; 52-53 Bournemouth News/Rex Features; 54 © Anton Gvozdikov/Shutterstock.com; 55 © Faraways/Shutterstock.com; 56-57 www.sell-my-photo.co.uk; 58-59 © NHPA/Photoshot; 60 © Dan Lee/Shutterstock.com; 62-63 (sp) Carol McCabe/Rex Features; 63 (t) © Alexander Kaludov/Shutterstock.com; 64 Rex Features; 65 © NHPA/Photoshot; 66-67 © NHPA/Photoshot; 68-69 Wayne Davies/Rex Features; 70 © Stuart Westmorland/Corbis; 72-73 © Oceans Image/Photoshot; 74 Gerard Lacz/Rex Features; 75 © tristan tan/Shutterstock.com; 76-77 David Jones/PA Archive/Press Association Images; 78 © Thomas Amby/Shutterstock.com; 79 © NHPA/Photoshot; 80 Rundstedt Rovillos/Solent News/Rex Features; 81 (l) Caters; (r) © NHPA/Photoshot; 82-83 Reuters/Daniel Munoz; 84 © Andy Rouse/Naturepl.com; 85 © NHPA/Photoshot; 86 © Aaron Amat/Shutterstock.com; 87 Action Press/Rex Features; 88 Gavin Rodgers/Rex Features; 89 Reuters/Yuri Maltsev; 90-91 © NHPA/Photoshot; 93 Getty Images; 94 © Fabien Monteil/Shutterstock.com; 95 © AdShooter/iStock.com; 96 Jamie Hall/Solent News/Rex Features; 97 © Prill Mediendesign und Fotografie/Shutterstock.com; 98 © Potapov Alexander/Shutterstock.com; 100-101 KeystoneUSA-Zuma/Rex Features; 102 Action Press/Rex Features; 103 (l) KPA/Zuma/Rex Features, (r) John O' Reilly/Rex Features; 104-105 © Bruce Coleman/Photoshot; 106 © Mixrinho/Shutterstock.com; 107 (t) © Thomas Amby/Shutterstock.com; 108-109 Reuters/China Daily China Daily Information Corp/CDIC; 110 Gerard Lacz/Rex Features; 111 © Rich Carey/Shutterstock.com; 112-113 Paul Lovelace/Rex Features; 116 © Wei-Chieh Wu/iStock.com; 117 NASA/Rex Features; 118-119 Newspix/Rex Features; 120 WestEnd6ı/Rex Features;